Small Thoughts For Big Change

21 Beliefs to Create Magic In Your Life

By
Sarah Carson
Shawn Carson and
Jess Marion

I0224609

Small Thoughts For Big Change: 21 Beliefs To Create Magic In Your Life

Copyright 2016 Sarah Carson, Shawn Carson, Jess Marion and Changing Mind Publishing. All rights reserved

All images produced with www.easel.ly.com

No part of this book may be reproduced in any manner whatsoever without written permission except in the case of brief quotations embedded in critical articles and reviews.

For further information please contact Changing Mind Publishing at 545 8th Avenue, Suite 930, New York, N.Y. 10018

Introduction and Welcome

Sometimes we make a small decision that has a huge and lasting impact on our life. Many years ago I decided to take an NLP course, simply because it sounded interesting. I had no idea at the time that this decision was to have an enduring and profound effect on my life. One aspect of NLP I learned about is called 'presuppositions'. Presuppositions are ideas and thoughts that we hold as being useful while coaching another person. I remember learning some of the basic "presups" very early on in my NLP course; to be completely frank, I put them aside as "nice" thoughts that didn't really fit with the other more important aspects of NLP. How wrong I was! Fast forward a few years and I began to see the deep value of these presuppositions in the personal transformation I was experiencing

You see, these small thoughts had created a big change in me and they can for you too!

These small thoughts are more than "nice words", or cute Facebook memes. They are more than affirmations or morning meditations. They are beliefs that can create magic in your life, and truly become the lenses through which you see the world "and everything thats in it."

The 21 presuppositions we have selected for this book (OK we have added a couple more) come from both NLP and HNLP, from Richard Bandler, John Grinder, Paul Watzlawick, John Overdurf, Julie Silverthorn, Gregory Bateson and many more. We thank them for their brilliance, and we delight in the knowledge that your small decision to pick up this book today may have a huge and lasting impact on your life.

Sarah Carson

How To Use This Book

Each page of this book gives you a belief, a useful thought, an alternative perspective for you to ponder and consider, based on the NLP and HNLP presuppositons

Take time to apply these new ways of thinking to your life whenever you can

Some of them will be eye opening in the moment, some may simply not apply, some may cause you to stop and think differently and some will change your life

At the end of the book we have included some "explorations" for you to play with. These may refer to specific presuppositions and a few include a number of presuppositions. Explore these and create some of your own too!

And finally, remember that Small Thoughts can create BIG Change

Connecting

The Meaining of your Communication is in the Response you get

A thousand years ago the warlike vikings were traveling the world. They didn't usually receive a warm welcome!

"Why doesn't anyone seem to like us?" they asked.

Of course it was because the vikings believed that they had to make everyone else lose in order to win. But in the end all they won were battles and scars.

The great Thomas Edison's first invention was an automatic voting machine for use in Congress. But it would have stopped corrupt politicians from taking bribes. So no-one would buy it.

Edison vowed to only invent things that people would want to buy!
A BRIGHT idea!

Whether you're persuading an audience, or negotiating a business deal, the REAL meaning of what you're saying lies in the space inbetween you and the other. Knowing this allows you to tailor your message based on their response.

After all, you might think your idea is the greatest, but if no-one else agrees you're wasting your time!

Blah blah

REMEMBER! Raising others up doesn't diminish you, you win when they win as well. Take responsibility for your communication. If they don't get it yet, you just haven't found the right way to say it yet!

We can't not communicate.
We are always communicating

Even when we are not speaking, our body is communicating in various ways.

Skin tone/blush

Gestures

Posture

Eye movements

Rate of breathing

Facial expression

This strange looking guy is called a "homunculus". This image has been around for hundreds of years and has been used to explain many things from our evolution to our human-ness.

hearing

seeing

tasting

We can also look at our friend as a reminder of our amazing senses and remind ourselves that it is through our senses that we take in ALL information.

smelling

feeling and touching

Our unconscious mind will always communicate first , so when we are open and aware then we can become better communicators, and change workers

There is no substitute for clear, open sensory channels

Visual

Auditory

Kinesthetic

Gustatory

Olfactory

Think of a dog... Perhaps you see a picture of a dog... Or hear it bark... Or say 'dog' to yourself... Or feel its fur... Or smell a doggy smell... Maybe you even imagined licking it (although I wouldn't advise that!). However you thought of the dog you used one of your senses. Every thought we have we use our senses to think!

The Wise Unconscious

No matter what you think you are

You are ALLWAYS

More than that

Behind Every Behavior Is A Positive Intention

Since we were babies we were motived to act in ways that we believed would help us

The athlete trains to become skilled at her or his sport because it meets their values. The spectator watches and cheers because it makes them feel good.

Even the angry boss has a positive intention. He may yell to relieve his own stress or because he believes it's the best way to motivate his staff

Sometimes our thoughts, feelings and behavior don't feel like that match who we are. Sometimes clients say that when they experience themselves it's like that part of them is a monster. It's not! The unconscious mind is acting and communicating with your best interest at heart, even if it is not the most resourceful way.

If you ever find your self behaving in a way you wish you didn't or feeling bad

Thank your unconscious mind and ask that part of you what the positive intention is. Your unconscious mind is giving you a gift in those moments.

We Make The Best Choices Available

Every living being makes the best choice available. Animals make choices to help them survive and flourish

You are genetically programmed to do the same. Your ancestors made the best choices available and now you are here!

Sometimes the choices people make are viewed as not being the best by others. Sometimes you might make choices that looking back you wish you hadn't

We make choices based on our states and those states are informed by our thoughts, memories, beliefs, values and behavior. Out of all of the possibilities available we choose what we feel is the best possible option for our survival and flourishing.

No one is broken
or needs to be
fixed
Everyone is doing
their good stuff and
their "bad" stuff
perfectly!
People
Work
Perfectly
If someone wants to
change then all we have
to to do is figure our
HOW they are doing
what they are doing...
...and change it!
(Yes...even
him!!)

You Have All The Resources You Need

You come from a long line of resourceful people over the centuries. If you didn't then you wouldn't be here now. You are by default wonderfully resourceful. You have a life time of experiences, learnings, emotions, memories and skills. There is nothing you can't achieve when you are as resourceful as you are. Any change you would like to make in your life is within your ability.

Changing and Learning

Some animals are born with most of the learnings they will ever need. That's not true for humans...

Human beings have so much to learn, you had to learn how to walk...

And you learned by falling over...

After all, LIVING IS LEARNING

...and getting back up again!

You can even learn from things you THINK you understand, by looking deeper

...or when there are things you don't understand... at first...

As you grew up you learned how to use your brain...

You never stop learning. You can learn most when things go wrong...

...and your body.

You got certificates to show how much you've learned

Then you started to teach others what you know... but...

Reality Is A Construction

Your experience of what is real is unique to you. You create it based on your thoughts, feelings, beliefs, values, and memories.

All of those filters influence how you interpret the information that comes in through your senses.

So consider, what reality do you want to construct for yourself?

Confusion Pre-Seeds Growth

The unconscious mind always learns first.

So if you are feeling confused this simply means that your unconscious mind has learned something new...

...and your conscious mind is yet to realize it!

All we are is...

 **CHANGING**

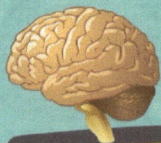

New brain cells are constantly being born, a process called 'neurogenesis'

The body begins the process of healing within a few minutes of the injury...

Emotions only last 90 seconds, Then they're gone...

Our senses are designed to respond to change. The human eye processes up to 12 pictures every second!

Thoughts are fleeting... It's estimated we have 50,000 every day, almost one every second!

We can change the way our genes work, a process called 'gene expression'

Relationships

In the movie "The Legend of Bagger Vance", Rannulph Junuh is a golfer who has "lost his swing". He is out one night practicing in his yard
Bagger Vance arrives and watches him. Eventually they talk and Junah asks him:
"Are you a caddy?"
"Well that depends…are you a golfer?"
Reality and Meaning are created through relationships
Put simply - Everything is relative.

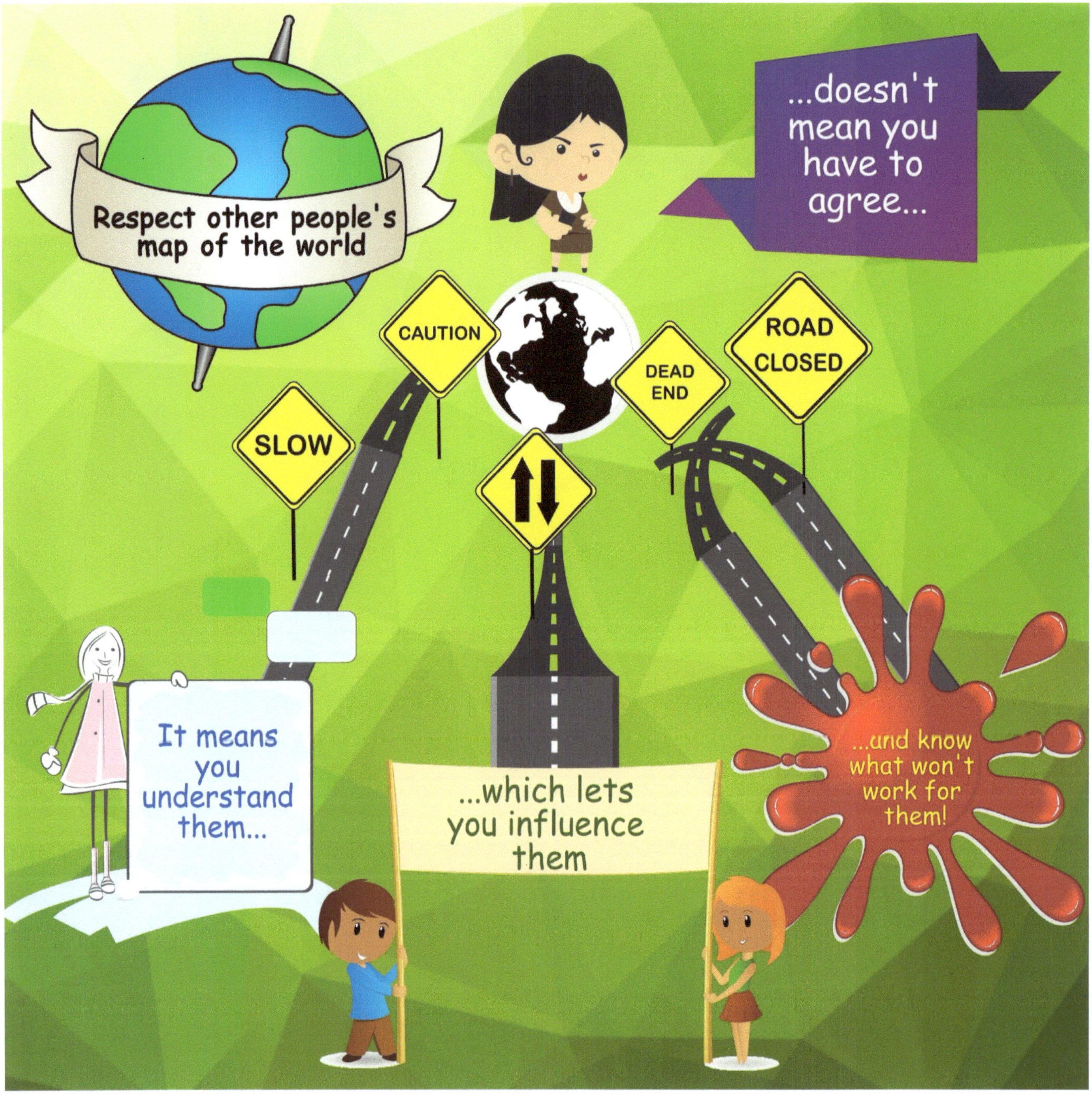
Respect other people's map of the world
...doesn't mean you have to agree...
CAUTION
SLOW
DEAD END
ROAD CLOSED
It means you understand them...
...which lets you influence them
...and know what won't work for them!

Everyone and Everything is Connected

Not long ago we could only speak to people within shouting distance, or send a letter or travel to see them by train (or horse and cart!)

BUY **24/7**

Now you can travel to the other side of the world by plane in hours, or buy something from a distant country with one click...

You can be connected to your family and friends no matter where they are through your smart phone...

You literally hold the world in your hand...

Even science says that you are connected to every particle in the Unverse through 'Quantum Entanglement'

These connection, what you say and how you act, can cause others to do, feel, or be their best based on YOUR actions. Choose your next words carefully, the world is watching!

Experiences

The Pendulum Pattern

Use a pendulum and find your "yes" and "no" direction

Think of an issue or problem and associate into it

Select a few presuppositions that "speak" to you

Select one presupposition and ask your unconscious mind if this is the best one to consider for your specific issue

Allow the pendulum to move to the "yes" or "no" direction

If the pendulum moves to "no" simply select an alternative presupposition

If the pendulum moves to "yes" then allow your unconscious mind to view the issue from this new perspective

Yes

No

The Daisy Pattern

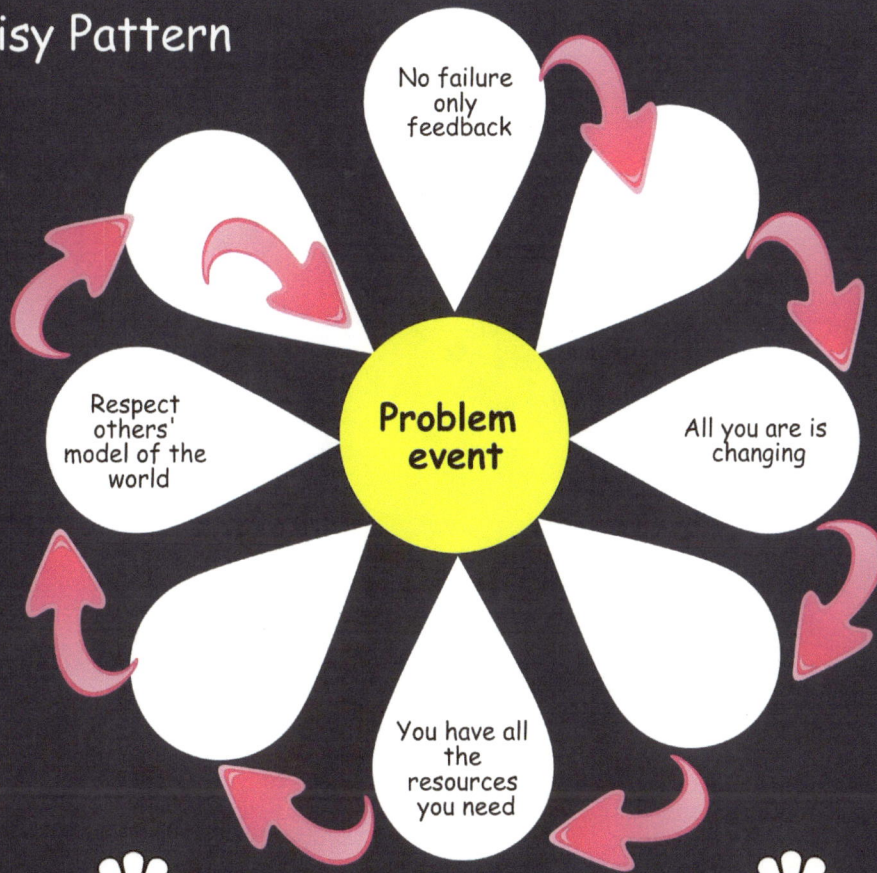

Problem event

No failure only feedback

All you are is changing

You have all the resources you need

Respect others' model of the world

Write out 4 presuppositions. Lay them in a circle with 4 blank "petals" in-between.

Think of a problem. Step into the center of the circle and associate into the issue just until you begin to feel it. Shake it off

Step into the space of your 1st presupposition. View your problem from this perspective. Notice how it is different

Step into your in-between "petal" and reset by shaking your body or thinking of something different

Repeat the two previous steps until you have visited all of your presuppositions

Now step into the center and notice how that problem has changed

This pattern is based on the work of Tim Hallbom and Suzie Smith

No Failure - Only Feedback exercise

Think of a time or situation that didn't go the way you had hoped.

Step into this specific moment, as though you are there experiencing it. Step in just enough so that you begin to actually feel the emotion.

Now step out and shake off that feeling

Now, from a more distanced perspective, consider everything that you learned from that experience

The things you would do differently, the alternative ways to approach it, the people who could have assisted, the lessons learned and the insight gained.

Step into these new learnings and embrace them.

Look back at that situation and notice how it is different now.

You can't not communicate - Exercise

Spend some time watching the TV or your computer

WITH THE SOUND OFF!!!

Choose a program which is unscripted and unrehearsed such as a talk show

Observe the body language of the people. Can you figure out some of their emotions?

Spend some time watching the TV or your computer

IN A LANGUAGE YOUR DON'T SPEAK!!

Choose a program which is unscripted and unrehearsed such as a talk show

Listen to the tone, pauses, tempo etc. of the language. Can you figure out some of their emotions?

Spend some time watching a couple in a cafe or restaurant

Observe their body language

Do you think this is a first date, old friends, or colleagues?

Remember, we can't not communicate... we are always communicating!

Mark out 4 spaces on the floor, one for each letter BEAT. Step into each space and access each element of the BEAT pattern to quickly and easily change your state. As each aspect peaks, anchor it by squeezing your thumb and finger. Repeat the chain enough times until you can access the state simply by firing the anchors and saying the letters.

If Something Isn't Working...Do something Different

B

Breathing/ Body

The quickest way to change your state is to change your physiology. So in this space, stand tall, with shoulders back. Alternatively take on the perfect posture for your desired outcome. Check in with your breathing and ensure it is calm and steady. Squeeze your thumb and forefinger together while saying "B" to anchor this.

E

Emotions

In this space check in with your emotions. If they are appropriate then go ahead and squeeze

your thumb and middle finger together while saying "E". If they are not appropriate, remember that every emotion only lasts around 60 seconds, so allow the emotion to subside and step into your desired emotion. When this is peaking anchor it with your thumb and middle finger while saying "E".

A

Awareness/Attention

Here, go into peripheral vision by softening and widening your gaze, drop your jaw and breathe steadily. this will allow you to widen your attention to find alternatives

Now squeeze together your thumb and ring finger while saying the letter 'A' to anchor this element.

T

Thoughts

Make a movie in your mind of exactly how you want to be in this moment. Add in a soundtrack and a fantastic title. By using your working memory you are creating the best possible thoughts for you in this moment. Anchor this by squeezing your thumb and pinkie together and saying the letter "T".

NO FAILURE ONLY FEEDBACK

Reality is a construction

There is no substitute for open sensory channels

People work perfectly

Confusion Pre-seeds Growth

If one person can do something then everyone can

The map is not the territory

People always make the best choices available to them

Behind every behavior is a positive intention

All We Are Is Changing

PRESUPPOSITIONS

We have all the resources we need

The Meaning of Your Communication Is the Response You Get

OF

Reality and meaning are created through relationships

LIVING IS LEARNING

All distinctions are made through our 5 senses

If what you are doing isn't working, do something different

Everything and Everyone is Interconnected

Respect others model of the world

NLP

WE ARE ALWAYS COMMUNICATING

Law of Requisite Variety. The person with the most flexibility...wins

No Matter What You Think You Are You Are ALLWAYS More Than That

Perception is learned

You Never Know How Far A Change Will Go

You Never Know How Far A Change Will Go

You Never Know How Far A Change Will Go

You Never Know How Far A Change Will Go

You Never Know How Far A Change Will Go

You Never Know How Far A Change Will Go

You Never Know How Far A Change Will Go

You Never Know How Far A Change Will Go

You Never Know How Far A Change Will Go

You Never Know How Far A Change Will Go

We hope you have enjoyed reading this book, playing with the experiences, considering these beliefs and pondering on the ideas. We know that you are already changing from having had this experience and now we wonder just how far this change will go because
... you never know...

Other Publications by the authors:

The Swish: An In Depth Look at this Powerful NLP Pattern. (NLP Mastery Series)
Shawn Carson and Jess Marion

The Visual Squash: An NLP Tool for Radical Change. (NLP Mastery Series)
Jess Marion and Shawn Carson

The Meta Pattern: The Ultimate Structure of Influence for Coaches, Hypnosis Practitioners, and Business Executives.
(NLP Mastery Series)
Sarah Carson and Shawn Carson

The BEAT Coaching System. (NLP Mastery Series)
Shawn Carson and Sarah Carson

Quit: The Hypnotist's Handbook to Running Effective Stop Smoking Sessions.
Jess Marion, Sarah Carson, Shawn Carson

Keeping the Brain in Mind: Practical Neuroscience for Coaches, Therapists, and Hypnosis Practitioners.
Shawn Carson, Melissa Tiers

Deep Trance Identification: Unconscious Modeling and Mastery for Hypnosis Practitioners, Coaches, and Everyday People.
Shawn Carson, Jess Marion, John Overdurf

Deep Trance Identification: The Companion Manual.
Shawn Carson, Jess Marion, John Overdurf

Tree of Life Coaching: Practical Secrets of the Kabbalah for Coaches and Hypnosis and NLP Practitioners.
Shawn Carson

I Quit: Stop Smoking Easily Through the Power of Hypnosis.
Jess Marion, Sarah Carson and Shawn Carson

HypnoGames For HypnoJunkies.
Sarah Carson, Shawn Carson and Jess Marion,

Call to Client
Jess Marion, Sarah Carson, Shawn Carson

The Reality Distortion Field: Change The World By Convincing Others To Share Your Dream
Shawn Carson

For further information please contact Changing Mind Publishing at 545 8th Avenue, Suite 930, New York, N.Y. 10018 or visit www.theintelligenthypnotist.com

www.ingramcontent.com/pod-product-compliance
Lightning Source LLC
Chambersburg PA
CBHW061050090426
42740CB00002B/100